Accelerated learning in the Literacy Hour

Year 4

Sue Garnett

Published by Hopscotch Educational Publishing Ltd, 29 Waterloo Place, Leamington Spa CV32 5LA (Tel: 01926 744227)

© 2002 Hopscotch Educational Publishing

Written by Susan Garnett
Series design by Blade Communications
Illustrated by Debbie Clark
Cover illustration by Debbie Clark
Printed by Clintplan, Southam

ISBN 1-904307-13-2

ACCELERATED LEARNING IN THE LITERACY HOUR

This series of books and the activity ideas are a direct result of the research into brain-based learning and multiple intelligences, how the brain works and how children learn. Howard Gardner sets out the results of this research in his books *Accelerated Learning in the Classroom* and *Accelerated Learning in Practice* (published by Network Educational Press Ltd). Information from his research and these books is given below.

Visual, Auditory and Kinaesthetic Learning (VAK)

People learn using their senses: their sense of hearing, sight and touch.

- 29% of us prefer to learn by seeing.
- 34% of us prefer to learn by hearing and using sound.
- 37% of us prefer to learn by doing.

It is important to know which is our preference, but it is just as important to learn to use the other senses too.

If we are to maximise children's learning, we should be aware of the children's strengths and provide them not only with activities that they prefer, but also give them access to all three types of learning so that they will learn new skills.

We remember:
- 20% of what we see
- 30% of what we hear
- 40% of what we say
- 50% of what we do
- 90% of what we see, hear, say and do.

Therefore, it is vital that you deliver lessons in such a way that there is variety, i.e. by using visual, auditory and kinaesthetic activities. You should provide input that covers all three types of learning. This may be done during the course of a lesson or over a series of lessons.

It is important that you provide a balanced curriculum covering the three types of learning just as you would provide a balanced diet.

Multiple Intelligences (MI)

Howard Gardner identified the Seven Plus One Intelligences (this has now become Nine Intelligences). He said that people have different types of intelligences and that they are better at some than others. All nine intelligences are important. All children are intelligent in some way.

The nine intelligences are:
- logical (Number/order smart)
- linguistic (Word smart)
- visual/spatial (Picture smart)
- interpersonal (People smart)
- intrapersonal (Myself smart)
- physical (Body smart)
- naturalistic (Naturalistic smart)
- musical (Music smart)
- spiritual.

Children benefit from a balance of activities in order to enhance their preferred learning style. But it is also important to introduce them to other types of learning to strengthen and develop the ones with which they are not as confident. Providing a range of activities and a balance of activities will maximise their learning.

A balanced approach to learning

Visual, auditory and kinaesthetic learning fit in really well with the Nine Intelligences.

Example

Lesson objective – to produce a poster in small groups advertising a wildlife park.
The children would be learning visually.
The children would also be using several of the Nine Intelligences, i.e. linguistic, visual/spatial, interpersonal and naturalistic.

What is this book?

This book is a teacher resource. It provides a series of ideas to use in the classroom that will develop and maximise children's learning.

It provides visual, auditory and kinaesthetic activities to achieve the text level objectives of the National Literacy Strategy.

It also includes references to the Nine Intelligences.

This book will help towards enabling ALL children to be successful. It helps you to reach all of the children more of the time.

How does this book work?

Each lesson plan contains a literacy objective (text level), a whole class starter activity, ideas for group work (visual, auditory and kinaesthetic activities) and a plenary session. Each lesson also contains three sheets:

Sheet 1
This is a model that you share with the children.

Sheet 2
This sheet gives information on the three activities (visual, auditory and kinaesthetic) you can use with the children to achieve the objective. You could split the children into groups according to their preferred learning style, or cover all the activities over a period of time. Children with special educational needs could cover the style they are most likely to be successful with.

Sheet 3
This is the children's worksheet. They may use it to make notes or plan their work.

If there are adult helpers in the class, they can work with a group of children on one of the objectives.

Recognising children's preferred learning styles

Below are lists of activities that the different types of learner enjoys doing. Over a period of time, teachers should try to ensure that children receive a balance from each list.

VISUAL LEARNERS

They learn best through seeing.

How can you recognise a visual learner?
They speak with their hands. They like to point things out. They speak rapidly.

What do they enjoy?
- Writing
- Drawing
- Computers
- OHPs
- Television
- Posters
- News reports
- Books
- Diaries
- Letters
- Key words
- Wall displays
- Films/videos
- Interactive whiteboards
- Interactive displays
- Arrow charts
- Flow charts
- Graphs
- Diagrams
- Pictures
- Mind maps

AUDITORY LEARNERS

They learn best through sound.

How can you recognise an auditory learner?
They like to hum, sing or whistle while doing activities.
They like to give and receive instructions verbally.

What do they enjoy?
- Audio tapes/CDs
- Radio programmes
- Circle time
- Hot seating
- Lectures
- Show and tell
- Debates/discussion
- School council
- Point of view
- Music and sound effects
- Interviews/interviewing
- Reporting
- Dance
- Drama

KINAESTHETIC LEARNERS

They learn best through movement.

How can you recognise a kinaesthetic learner?
They like to move about the classroom and touch things.
They get restless sitting down. They like physical activities.
They like to demonstrate or model. They fidget.

What do they enjoy?
- Role play and dressing up
- Show and tell
- Making things
- Modelling and collage
- Murals
- Puppet and mask making
- Flap books and concertina books
- Outdoor lessons
- Field trips
- Outdoor pursuits
- PE
- Dance
- Gym
- Music and Movement
- Brain gym
- Performances

How to find out what type of learner a child is

On the next page (page 6) is a questionnaire. The children can either be given this to complete themselves or they can be helped by an adult to complete it.

The key to the questionnaire is given on page 7. For example, if the answer given to the first question by a child is 'Yes' then that indicates 'kinaesthetic'.

The results may show that the child has a dominant learning style or it may show that he or she has several learning styles.

The idea is to provide you, the teacher, with valuable information about the children so that you are better able to help them with their learning.

What kind of learner am I?

Name _____   Class _____

1. I like making things.	Yes	No
2. I like watching films.	Yes	No
3. I like listening to music.	Yes	No
4. I like listening to story tapes.	Yes	No
5. I like designing posters.	Yes	No
6. I like acting.	Yes	No
7. I like sport and playing out.	Yes	No
8. I like drawing.	Yes	No
9. I like lessons outdoors.	Yes	No
10. I like school trips.	Yes	No
11. I like dancing.	Yes	No
12. I like writing.	Yes	No
13. I like talking.	Yes	No
14. I like show and tell.	Yes	No
15. I like speaking in front of others.	Yes	No
16. I like debating and discussing.	Yes	No
17. I like drawing diagrams.	Yes	No
18. I like looking at the blackboard.	Yes	No
19. I like using whiteboards.	Yes	No
20. I like to talk while I work.	Yes	No
21. I like moving about.	Yes	No
22. I like reading.	Yes	No

What kind of learner am I? (Answer key)

1. K
2. V
3. A
4. A
5. V
6. K
7. K
8. V
9. K
10. K
11. K
12. V
13. A
14. A
15. A
16. A
17. V
18. V
19. V
20. A
21. K
22. V

Count up how many of each type they have.

> **Example**
>
> Jack Barnes   Class 6
>
> Visual = 0
> Auditory = 3
> Kinaesthetic = 6
>
> Dominant learning style = kinaesthetic

If a child circles all the yes answers, then they have no preferred learning style.

If they circle yes to 1, 6, 7, 9, 10, 11, 21 then they are a kinaesthetic learner.

If they circle yes to 2, 5, 8, 12, 17, 18, 19, 22 then they are a visual learner.

If they circle yes to 3, 4, 13, 14, 15, 16, 20 then they are an auditory learner.

Most children have a dominant learning style. If you give them the appropriate type of learning activity, then they will learn. For example, give a kinaesthetic learner things to make and things to do.

It is also important to give children a variety of activities not just those from their own preferred learning style in order that they develop new skills.

Children can be told what kind of learner they are. If they understand how they learn best, they can help themselves.

Characters

Whole class starter

Literacy objective

- To create a character sketch focusing on small detail.

What you need

- Photocopies of pages 10, 12 and 13
- Sheets of paper
- Colouring/drawing materials
- Storybook and/or video of Robin Hood

- Give each child a copy of the character description sheet on page 10 or display it on an OHP or interactive whiteboard.

- Tell the children that they are going to work on character sketches.

- Read the description with the children. Tell them that this is a character sketch. Explain that a character sketch is useful when writing a story as it gives the reader a mental picture at the beginning of a story.

- Ask the children the following questions.

  - Who is the character in the story?
  - This story is set a long time ago. How do we know?
  - What does the character look like?
  - Was the king wealthy?
  - How had he become wealthy?
  - Did the townspeople like the king?
  - What evidence is there to say that he was not liked?
  - Do you think he is a likeable character?
  - How does the writer get the reader to dislike the character?

8

Independent/group work

From the activities on page 11 either:

- select the most appropriate activity for each child/group according to whether they are kinaesthetic, auditory or visual learners and organise three separate working groups;

or

- begin with the kinaesthetic activity for the whole class, then progress to the auditory and finally the visual activity over several lessons.

Tell the children that they are now going to work on characters.

The kinaesthetic learners will need:
sheets of paper and copies of the character description on page 10.

The auditory learners will need:
a storybook and/or video of Robin Hood and copies of pages 13.

The visual learners will need:
a storybook and/or video of Robin Hood and copies of page 12.

Plenary

Share the results from the activities.

- What adjectives did the children use to describe their characters?
- What have they written about their character that would make the reader like him/her?
- How were the adjectives and similes important?
- Write the adjectives on the board. Ask the children to tell you which are the 'premiership' words, i.e. the best words. For example, 'ruthless' is a premiership word, 'nice' is not. Ask some of the children to come to the board and draw a circle around them. Tell them that they should try to use 'premiership' words in their own writing. Look at some of the simple adjectives and discuss 'premiership' alternatives, such as kind – thoughtful, considerate.
- The children could use thesauruses to find alternative 'premiership' adjectives.

Extension activity

History – You could link this work with a topic you are doing in history about famous characters – for example, Julius Caesar, Tutankhamun, Henry VIII. Ask the children to write a character sketch of a famous person from the period you are studying.

The King of Budespan

The King of Budespan reigned for 50 years. He reigned without a wife and family. He reigned with fear and dread.

He wore a long gold cloak sewn with golden thread. He wore a crown encrusted with diamonds and sparkling jewels, which glittered more than the sun, and on every finger he wore gold rings the size of marbles.

King Budespan had a mouth that never smiled and a long black moustache that drooped downwards. His eyes were as black as the darkest dungeon, never showing fear or sadness. In his whole life he never shed one tear, not even when the townsfolk were struck down with the plague and died one by one.

If the townsfolk were late paying their taxes, he would shout, 'Off with their heads!' If they were caught poaching animals from his land, he would have their hands cut off, never once listening to their cries that they were dying of hunger.

He cared for no one but himself. And when he died no one came to his funeral and no one brought flowers to his grave. His castle was left to ruin until all that remained was a pile of stones, a memory of a man with a heart of stone, like the stones from his castle.

Kinaesthetic learning

(Physical, Intrapersonal, Linguistic, Visual/Spatial)

Draw the character

- Tell the children that they are going to work on their own to draw and label the character of the king from the story.

- Give them copies of the character description of the king of Budespan and some sheets of paper. Ask them to draw the king and then label the drawing with words from the text, for example 'long black moustache'.

- When the children have finished, invite them to show and compare their drawings. How are they different? Do all the pictures make the king look mean?

Auditory learning

(Kinaesthetic, Interpersonal, Linguistic)

Create new characters

- Tell the children that they are going to work together to think up some new characters for the story, for example a hero and/or a villager. To help them, they can read the story of Robin Hood (which has similar characters) or watch a video.

- Provide the children with the list of adjectives from page 13 to help them create their new character.

- Ask the children to practise acting out their new characters, for example 'My name is Bill. I'm a villager. I work hard on the land and look after my family...'

- After preparation, let the children act out their characters to the rest of the class.

- Invite the class to say whether the character is likeable or not, with reasons.

- Write down the words that the children use to describe the characters.

Visual learning

(Visual/Spatial, Linguistic, Intrapersonal)

Write a character sketch

- Tell the children that they are going to work on their own to write a character sketch of a hero or heroine (the opposite sort of character to the king in the story).

- They can read the story or watch the video of Robin Hood, which has similar characters, to help them.

- On a copy of page 12, they should make some notes about their new character.

- Then they should use the notes to write a full character sketch.

My character

Name _____

What he/she looks like

- _____
- _____
- _____
- _____
- _____
- _____
- _____
- _____

His/her character

- _____
- _____
- _____
- _____

THINK ABOUT...
- Interesting adjectives
- Mannerisms

Evidence of his/her character

- _____
- _____
- _____
- _____

WORD BANK

tunic	old boots	cloak

kind	thoughtful	honest
friendly	brave	hardworking
cheerful	bold	trustworthy

works hard
looks after his/her family
plays with his/her children
shares what he/she has
gives things away
fights cruel people
stands up for what is right

Words to describe characters

kind	thoughtful
honest	happy
loyal	cheerful
bold	hardworking
cheerful	strong
brave	friendly
heroic	trustworthy

Playscripts

Whole class starter

Literacy objective

- To create playscripts using known stories.

What you need

- Photocopies of pages 16 and 18
- Old socks, felt and wool
- Scissors and glue
- Tape recorder/dictaphone

- Give each child a copy of the playscript on page 16 or display it on an OHP or interactive whiteboard.

- Tell the children that they are going to learn how to create playscripts. What do they think a playscript is? Encourage them to share their ideas. Say that they may have some more ideas about playscripts after reading one called 'The Ugly Duckling'.

- Read through the play 'The Ugly Duckling'. Explain that this is a playscript.

- Ask some of the children to take the parts of the characters and read through the playscript again.

- Now ask the following questions.

  – This is a playscript. How is it different from a story?
    - It is set out differently.
    - It has the names of characters down the left-hand side of the page.
    - It has information about how the characters speak or move.
    - Whenever a different character speaks, the writer starts a new line.

  – Have you heard this play before?
  – How is the play different to the story?
  – Who are the characters in the play?

- Tell the children that there are brackets in the playscript. Challenge them to find them all, then underline or circle them. What are the brackets for? (They tell us how the character is moving, or how they are speaking.) What do the children notice about the words in the brackets? (They are all doing words.)

- If you feel the children can grasp the concept, talk about the term 'stage directions' and about the roles of the director, the stage manager, the prompt and so on.

Independent/group work

From the activities on page 17 either:

- select the most appropriate activity for each child/group according to whether they are kinaesthetic, auditory or visual learners and organise three separate working groups;

or

- begin with the kinaesthetic activity for the whole class, then progress to the auditory and finally the visual activity over several lessons.

Tell the children that they are now going to work on their own playscripts.

The kinaesthetic learners will need:
old socks, felt, wool, scissors and glue.

The auditory learners will need:
a tape recorder or dictaphone.

The visual learners will need:
copies of 'My playscript' (page 18).

Plenary

Show the results from each activity.

- Which fairytale did the children recreate as a play?
- What problems did they have in creating the play? How did they resolve them?
- Who were the characters in their plays?
- What words did they put in brackets?
- How did the words in brackets help the reader?
- Was it easier or harder writing a playscript than writing a story? Why?
- What have the children learned about playscripts?
- How would they improve the play if they did it again?

Extension activities

Literacy – Ask the children to read a story that they have written this term and convert it into a playscript.

RE – You could link playscripts to stories you have read in RE – for example, the birth of Jesus, Noah's Ark, or the story of the loaves and fishes. Ask the children to convert one of the stories into a play.

The Ugly Duckling

Narrator: A duck laid her eggs in a bush by the river. One by one the eggs hatched. The last one to hatch was different from the rest.

Mother Duck: *(Looking at the ugly duckling.)* Ooh, what an ugly duckling!

Narrator: The ugly duckling grew bigger and bigger. He looked so different to the rest. The other birds teased him and hurt him.

Cockerel: *(Pecking the ugly duckling.)* What an ugly duckling you are!

Ugly Duckling: You are all very mean. *(Then running away.)*

Narrator: He hid himself away for many months. Soon autumn came.

Ugly Duckling: *(Looking upwards.)* What are those things in the sky?

Narrator: The things in the sky were swans. The ugly duckling hid in the bush until spring came and the swans returned. He swam over to them.

Swan: Look! A new swan!

Narrator: The ugly duckling was afraid. He didn't realise they meant him.

Ugly Duckling: *(Shakily.)* Please don't kill me!

Narrator: Then he looked at his reflection in the water and couldn't believe what he saw.

Ugly Duckling: *(Shouting.)* I'm a swan! I'm a swan!

Narrator: The ugly duckling was not an ugly duckling after all. He was a swan – a beautiful swan.

Kinaesthetic learning

(Physical, Interpersonal, Linguistic)

Sock puppet play

- Tell the children that they are going to work in groups to make some sock puppets and then act out a fairytale using them, such as Little Red Riding Hood.

- Read the chosen fairytale to the children. Ask them to choose a character they wish to play.

- Help the children to make a sock puppet of their chosen character. Provide them with socks, felt for eyes, nose and mouth, and wool for hair.

- After practice, invite the children to perform their puppet play to the rest of the class.

Auditory learning

(Interpersonal, Linguistic)

Tape a fairytale

- Tell the children that they are going to retell the fairytale of Goldilocks and the Three Bears in a radio play version.

- Read the story to the children. Ask them to choose a character they wish to play.

- Help the children to practise their performance of the story and then tape it on audio cassette.

- Play the tape to the rest of the class.

Visual learning

(Visual/spatial, Intrapersonal, Linguistic)

Convert a fairytale into a play

- Tell the children that they are going to work on their own to convert the fairytale of Cinderella into a play.

- Ask them to think of all the characters in the story.

- They should write their list of characters and their ideas for what happens in the story on a copy of the 'My playscript' sheet on page 18.

- Then they should write their play on a new sheet of paper. When they have finished, photocopy some of their plays for the rest of the class to join in with.

My playscript

Title

_____

Characters

_____

_____

_____

_____

_____

What happens

_____

_____

_____

_____

_____

_____

WORD BANK

Characters
Cinderella
Ugly Sisters
Fairy Godmother
Prince

Places
cottage
palace
castle

Stage directions
shouting
brushing the floor
crying
angrily
happily
sadly
running as fast as she can
holding hands

THINK ABOUT...
• How you will set out
  the play:
  – characters on the
    left-hand side
  – new line when
    someone speaks

Experiencing history

Literacy objective

- To write independently, linking own experiences to situations in historical stories.

What you need

- Photocopies of pages 21 and 23
- Information books about important events/periods in history
- Objects connected to historical events
- A computer with a word processing program

Whole class starter

- Give each child a copy of the 'Boadicea and the Romans' sheet on page 21 or display it on an OHP or interactive whiteboard.

- Tell the children that they are going to work on stories from history.

- Read the story 'Boadicea and the Romans'. Tell the children that this is a story from history. It is the story of Queen Boadicea and is set during Roman times (55AD). Explain that it is written as if from the point of view of a Roman soldier from the time. Tell the children something about the Romans if they have not studied them in history.

- Ask the children the following questions.

  - When did the story take place?
  - Where did the story take place?
  - Why was Queen Boadicea so frightening?
  - How did the writer feel?
  - Have you ever been in a frightening situation?
  - What was it and how did you feel?

- Explain that they are now going to write about a period of history as if they had been there and experienced the event for themselves. Read the story of the soldier and Boadicea again. What writing features has the author used to help make the story interesting?

- Think about other feelings. Make a list on the board: fear, happiness, sadness, excitement, anger and so on.

- Discuss situations when the children have experienced these feelings, for example when a pet died or they had a fight with someone. (You might need to be diplomatic with some children here.)

- Now talk about the period of history you have been looking at. Try to relate each feeling to that period of history. For example, in a topic on the Roman invaders, think about their feelings as they were sailing across the sea to England (fear) and attending a tournament in the arena (excitement).

Extension activities

History/Literacy – Ask the children to stick their stories into a scrapbook with the title 'Famous moments in history'. The book could be put into the library for other children to consult.

The children could write a recount about a special event they remember then relate it to a time in history and write a story about that – for example, 'My birthday – Queen Victoria's birthday'; 'When my auntie got married – When Henry VIII got married'.

Independent/group work

From the activities on page 22 either:

- select the most appropriate activity for each child/group according to whether they are kinaesthetic, auditory or visual learners and organise three separate working groups;

or

- begin with the kinaesthetic activity for the whole class, then progress to the auditory and finally the visual activity over several lessons.

Tell the children they are now going to work on stories in history using their own experiences to help them.

The kinaesthetic learners will need:
information books about an important event in history, tea bags, hot water, A4 paper, copies of 'My historical story' on page 23.

The auditory learners will need:
information books about an important battle in history and copies of 'My historical story' on page 23.

The visual learners will need:
information books about an important event in history, copies of 'My historical story' on page 23 and a word processing program (if available).

Plenary

Share the results from the activities.

- How did it help the children to do the activity if they had not experienced something like this before?
- Why was it necessary to find out about the event before they wrote about it?
- Could they write about an historical story without knowing the facts? Why not?
- Why is research so important?
- What did the children do to help them imagine what the experience may have been like?
- What is the difference between reading a history book and listening to a retelling? Which is more exciting and why?

Boadicea and the Romans

When I was young, I was a soldier in the Roman army. I was a strong soldier and proud to be one of Caesar's men. We travelled around the world conquering other lands. I was a foot soldier but we had archers, too, and horsemen.

When I was 19, we sailed across the sea to England. Caesar wanted to conquer the land and make it his. We had many battles with the Britons and they did not give in easily.

One of the most difficult battles was against Queen Boadicea. The general led us to where the battle would take place and we waited in silence for her to arrive with her army. Suddenly, she appeared over the top of the hill riding a chariot pulled by two strong horses. The chariot had huge knives fixed to its wheels to cut down her enemies.

We heard shouts from her men as they came towards us. I was afraid because we had never seen a woman like this before. Then I looked around at my legion. We wore armour to protect us and we carried swords and shields. We had never lost a battle. Then the general shouted 'Charge!' We set off running across the field shouting as loud as we could. My heart beat like a drum but I had the men with me and I felt brave. The battle was bloody and we lost many men, but we won. Once again we were victorious!

Kinaesthetic learning

(Intrapersonal, Physical, Linguistic, Logical, Spiritual)

Make an old manuscript

- Tell the children that they are going to work on their own to produce an old manuscript on a topic such as Howard Carter finding the tomb of Tutankhamun.

- Give the children some books about the chosen historical event to look at.

- Make some old parchment by dipping a tea bag in hot water and dragging it all the way across a piece of paper several times.

- While the paper is drying, ask the children make some notes on a copy of page 23 about the special event. For example 'I opened the door slowly. I was amazed and excited by what I saw.'

- To help them imagine what it felt like, ask them to think of a time when they saw something amazing, such as Christmas morning snow!

- When the paper has dried they should use a black fibre-tipped pen to write what happened and sign it in the name of the famous person.

Auditory learning

(Intrapersonal, Linguistic, Logical, Spiritual)

Retell the story

- Tell the children that they are going to work on their own to retell a famous battle in history as if it has just happened, such as the Battle of Hastings.

- Give the children some books about the event and period to read.

- Encourage them to imagine what it feels like to be in a battle.

- Help them to use their senses to describe the scene. For example, 'I was at the Battle of Hastings. I could see... I could hear... I felt...'

- Ask the children to make notes on a copy of 'My historical story' on page 23 to help them.

- Invite them to retell the event to the rest of the class as if it has just happened.

Visual learning

(Intrapersonal, Visual/Spatial, Spiritual, Logical)

Rewrite the story

- Tell the children that they are going to work on their own to word process a recount of a special event in history, such as 'When I met King...', 'The Black Death' or 'The Fire of London'.

- Give the children some books about the event and period to read.

- Encourage the children to try to relate the historical event to some feeling they have had before, for example how they felt when they were ill (which relates to the Black Death).

- Give out copies of 'My historical story' on page 23 to help the children.

- Ask the children to word process their recount, including editing it.

My historical story

Make your notes inside the spiral. Turn the page as you write.

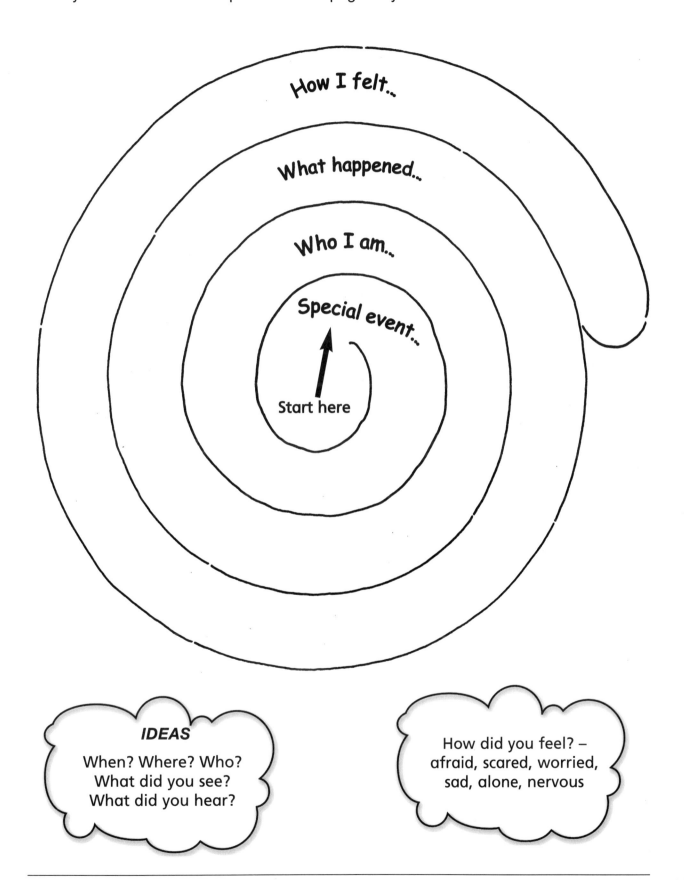

IDEAS

When? Where? Who?
What did you see?
What did you hear?

How did you feel? –
afraid, scared, worried,
sad, alone, nervous

Media reports

Whole class starter

Literacy objective

- To produce a news report.

What you need

- Photocopies of pages 26 and 28
- Tape recorder/dictaphone
- Large pieces of paper
- Newspaper
- Glue

- Give each child a copy of the newspaper report on page 26 or display it on an OHP or interactive whiteboard.

- Tell the children that they are going to work on newspaper reports.

- Share some newspaper pages with the children if they are not familiar with such reports. Look at the types of stories that are in newspapers. Draw the children's attention to the layout of a story, for example the headline, an introduction, photo captions, information and, perhaps, a quotation.

- Read the report, 'Cyclists not safe!' Look at the features of this newspaper report: the headline, introduction, subheading, photograph and caption, information and quotations. Discuss them with the children.

- The report answers four of the 'W' questions. Ask the children the following questions.

  - **What** is the report about?
  - **Where** is it taking place?
  - **Who** is it about?
  - **When** is it happening?
  - What are facts? What are opinions? Find examples in the text.
  - What is the headline? Why is it important? Why are short headlines better than long ones?
  - Find the quotations.
  - How is the report laid out?
  - The report is written in paragraphs. How many paragraphs are there? When do you begin a new paragraph?

- Tell the children they are going to create a news report together about the danger of school trips.
- First, list their ideas – road accidents, the danger of being in or near water, the danger of wild animals.
- Now draw the template for a newspaper report on the board (see page 28). Choose one of the ideas and ask them to give you a headline, intro and story. As they tell you the story, bit by bit, demonstrate writing it on the board in the template.

Independent/group work

From the activities on page 27 either:

- select the most appropriate activity for each child/group according to whether they are kinaesthetic, auditory or visual learners and organise three separate working groups;

or

- begin with the kinaesthetic activity for the whole class, then progress to the auditory and finally the visual activity over several lessons.

Tell the children they are going to work on their own newspaper reports.

The kinaesthetic learners will need:
large pieces of paper, newspapers and glue.

The auditory learners will need:
a tape recorder/dictaphone.

The visual learners will need:
copies of 'My news report' on page 28.

Plenary

Share the results from the activities.

- Ask some of the children to read out their reports. Did they include the four 'W's?
- What difference does it make if one of the four 'W's is missing? Do they notice any particular order that the four 'W's appear in?
- Now ask the children to hold up their reports. Check that they followed the necessary layout with a headline, photo, intro, caption, quote and text in columns. Why do they think reports are laid out in this way?

Extension activity

Literacy – Write possible headlines on pieces of card (for example, 'Midsummer Madness', 'Nowhere to go', 'School on red alert', 'Creepy Crawlies', 'No time to lose', 'Only the strongest survive', 'Head to head'). Invite the children to choose a card. Ask them what they think the report will be about.

THE DAILY SHOUT

23 November

Cyclists not safe!

This year there have been many more children receiving hospital treatment after having accidents on their bicycles.

One local hospital believes that the increase is a direct result of children not wearing helmets while they are riding their bicycles.

Doctor Jane Harding of Brumpton Hospital is worried about the growing problem.

"Last week," she told a Daily Shout reporter, "I attended to ten children who had been injured after falling off their bicycles. Six had head injuries and one is in a coma. Unless something is done about it we will see more deaths on the road."

Dr Jane Harding blames the injuries on children not wearing cycle helmets.

Dad takes the blame

Harry Parker, aged eight, was hit by a car last Friday. He was not wearing a helmet. Harry suffered concussion and was kept in hospital for two days. His father, Sam Parker, told us, 'We never thought about buying Harry a helmet. We never thought he'd need one. He won't be getting back on his bicycle until we've bought him one!'

Kinaesthetic learning

(Interpersonal, Intrapersonal, Physical, Logical)

Cut out and re-use newspaper stories

- Tell the children that they are going to work on their own and in pairs to produce a news report (using headline and photos from a newspaper).

- Prior to the lesson, cut out and photocopy suitable headlines and photographs from newspapers.

- Ask the children to choose one headline and photograph. Give each child a large piece of paper and ask them to stick the headline and photograph on it in the appropriate places.

- Have written up somewhere the four 'W's for them to see.

- They should discuss with a partner what their story might be about and think about the four 'W's. They should then write their report.

Auditory learning

(Interpersonal, Logical, Linguistic)

Make a radio report

- Tell the children that they are going to work in pairs to prepare a radio report on an incident involving a dangerous place, such as railways, canals or motorways.

- Each pair should choose a dangerous place and think of a story about something that could have happened there.

- Have written up somewhere the four 'W's for them to see.

- They should work together in their pairs on their story to describe what happened and give a quote from someone involved. They then record it on a recorder or dictaphone.

- In pairs, the children play back or read out their final radio report.

Visual learning

(Visual/Spatial, Intrapersonal, Linguistic)

Write a newspaper report

- Tell the children that they are going to work on their own to write their own newspaper report about potential dangers in the home, such as electricity, hot water, open windows, cookers and bunkbeds.

- Ask the children to decide on a danger and make notes on it. Encourage them to use 'W' questions to help them.

- Ask the children to write the final report on a copy of the sheet 'My news report' on page 28. (You could enlarge this sheet to A3 size.) They should think of a headline for their report and write in paragraphs. Encourage them to draw a picture and write a caption for it.

Name _____

My news report

Settings (science fiction)

Literacy objective

- To develop the use of settings.

What you need

- Photocopies of pages 31 and 33
- Paper – white, crêpe, sugar
- Glitter
- Paint
- Scissors and glue
- Sticky labels
- Tape recorder/dictaphone
- Blue sugar paper
- White chalk
- Silver and white wax crayons
- Charcoal

Whole class starter

- Give each child a copy of the Planet Triton story starter on page 31 or display it on an OHP or interactive whiteboard.

- Tell the children that they are going to work on settings. What do they think is meant by 'story setting'? Encourage them to share their ideas. Explain that they may have some more ideas about settings after sharing a text together called 'Dawn Raid on Planet Triton'.

- Read the text. Point out that this is a setting for a science fiction story.

- Now ask the children the following questions.

  - How do we know that this is a science fiction story? (It is set in the future; different planet; it uses technical/scientific language.)
  - Where is the story set?
  - What year is it?
  - What happens?
  - What do you think will happen next?

- Spend some time focusing on the language in the extract. Challenge the children to find evidence of scientific language, then encourage them to think of some of their own. The writer also uses lots of adjectives. Ask the children to find them. Why are adjectives useful when writing a setting? Finally, tell the children to shut their eyes. Can they imagine the planet? How do they think the writer enables them to do this?

- Re-examine the meaning of 'story setting'. Why is it important to know where a story is set? How might this help the reader? Does the reader need to know a lot about the setting or just a minimum of details? Does this depend on the kind of story it is? Ask the children to suggest some titles of stories they have read where the setting was very important to the story (for example, *The Lion, the Witch and the Wardrobe* by C S Lewis).

- Tell the children that they are now going to do more activities about story settings.

Extension activity

Literacy – Read the first few pages of a book that describes an unusual setting. Then tell the children to draw their own idea for what the setting looks like. When they have done this, ask them to compare their drawing with a partner's.

Independent/group work

From the activities on page 32 either:

- select the most appropriate activity for each child/group according to whether they are kinaesthetic, auditory or visual learners and organise three separate working groups;

or

- begin with the kinaesthetic activity for the whole class, then progress to the auditory and finally the visual activity over several lessons.

Tell the children that they are going to work on science fiction settings.

The kinaesthetic learners will need:
white paper, coloured crêpe and sugar paper, glitter, paints, scissors, glue and sticky labels.

The auditory learners will need:
copies of 'Science fiction settings' on page 33 and a tape recorder/dictaphone.

The visual learners will need:
copies of 'Science fiction settings' on page 33, blue sugar paper, white chalk, silver and white wax crayons and charcoal.

Plenary

Share the results from the activities.

- What have the children learned about settings?
- Why are adjectives so important when describing settings?
- How do the children know when they have successfully described a setting?
- Ask some of the children to read out/show and describe their setting. Ask the others to tell you the words they have heard that show it is science fiction, for example 'lazer' and 'supersonic'. Why are these words important when writing sci-fi? What would happen if we didn't use words like these?

Dawn Raid on Planet Triton

In the year 3000, Earthlings landed on the planet Triton. There was no life there and there never had been. It was a hot, dry land. The mountains were rocky and the colour of rust. Jagged volcanic rocks covered the land. Pools of bubbling lava still wound their way down the mountainsides. The sky was a ruby red from morning till night. Even the six suns were red and fiery.

In just two years, the Earthlings had built themselves a domed city from which they would never leave. It had houses, shops and lazer parks. They drove around in supersonic jets and the children had their school lessons at home from telepathic robots. Life was perfect ... that is until the dawn raids in the year 3003.

At precisely 4am, as dawn was breaking, a UFO was seen circling the planet. It was the size of a house and the shape of a cigar. A ring of flashing lights spun around its middle. It had flashing searchlights which lit the planet below like golden beams. By 4.05am there were hundreds of them circling the night sky like fireflies, bobbing and weaving, swooping and diving.

At 4.45am, as the suns peeped their heads over the horizon, the UFOs had landed. This was the first dawn raid!

Kinaesthetic learning

(Visual/Spatial, Linguistic, Intrapersonal, Naturalistic, Physical)

Make a collage

- Tell the children that they are going to work on their own to make a collage of planet Triton, developing further on what they already know.

- Provide sheets of white paper, coloured crêpe paper and sugar paper, glitter, paints, scissors and glue for the children to work with.

- After the children have made the collage, ask them to use sticky labels or pieces of white paper to write further information about the setting, for example 'the shops have jet landing pads.'

- Invite the children to show their collages to the rest of the class. Discuss if the collages look like the setting in the story.

Auditory learning

(Interpersonal, Linguistic, Logical, Naturalistic)

Tape a radio message

- Tell the children that they are going to work together to imagine that they are astronauts landing on 'Steam Planet'.

- Ask them to use the words on 'Science fiction settings' (page 33) to describe the planet to the people back on Earth. Together, ask them to think of sentences using the words provided.

- Invite the children to take it in turns to tape a sentence or two each onto a dictaphone or tape. Play the descriptive sentences to the rest of the class.

Visual learning

(Intrapersonal, Visual/Spatial, Linguistic, Physical, Naturalistic)

Making pictures

- Tell the children that they are going to work on their own to draw a picture of 'The Ice Planet' using the words on 'Science fiction settings' (page 33).

- Provide them with blue sugar paper, white chalk and silver and white wax crayons. Ask them to label the picture with charcoal.

- When they have completed their pictures, ask the children to use the picture and the words to write the setting for a story.

Science fiction settings

STEAM PLANET	ICE PLANET
Towering trees	Icy cold land
Exotic plants	Frozen lakes
Brightly coloured plants	Silvery white sky
Gigantic leaves	Jagged mountains
Strange plants	Glaciers like white icing
Poisonous flowers	Glittering caves
Dripping water	Ice caverns
Hot and humid	Silvery pools
Life form	Icicles like daggers
Green skin	No night
Hands like leaves	Icy blue sun
Bodies like snakes	No living thing
Feet like monkeys	

Extended stories

Literacy objective

- To collaborate with others to write stories in chapters.

What you need

- Photocopies of pages 36 and 38
- A4 ruled paper
- A4 plain paper
- A2 plain paper
- Glue
- Musical instruments
- Strips of A3 paper
- Sticky tape

Whole class starter

- Give each child a copy of 'Animal mad' on page 36 or display it on an OHP or interactive whiteboard.

- Tell the children that they are going to be working on longer stories with chapters. Have they read any of these? Can they name them?

- Read the 'Animal Mad' story from page 36 with the children. Explain that this is a longer story. Tell them that this page sets out an explanation of the contents of four chapters in a longer story about a boy called Josh. The story itself would, of course, be much longer than what they see here. Say that in a longer story each chapter contains a separate part of the story and probably has a different theme.

- Ask the children the following questions.

  – What is the story about?
  – What is the theme of the story?
  – How many chapters are there?
  – How did the writer decide how to split the story into chapters?
  – What other chapters could the writer have included?

- Ask the children to take out their reading books. Ask some of them to tell you and the others about their reading book – the title, the number of chapters and the titles of the chapters. What does the class notice about the chapters? (They might be linked, follow on or have a theme.)

Independent/group work

From the activities on page 37 either:

- select the most appropriate activity for each child/group according to whether they are kinaesthetic, auditory or visual learners and organise three separate working groups;

or

- begin with the kinaesthetic activity for the whole class, then progress to the auditory and finally the visual activity over several lessons.

Tell the children that they are going to work on a longer story.

The kinaesthetic learners will need:
A4 ruled paper, A4 plain paper, A2 plain paper, copies of 'My longer story' on page 38 and glue.

The auditory learners will need:
a variety of musical instruments.

The visual learners will need:
strips of A3 paper, copies of 'My longer story' on page 38 and sticky tape.

Plenary

Share the results from the activities.

- How is a longer story different from an ordinary story?
- Was it easier to write a longer story than the children thought?
- Did the finished result look more like a real book? Why?
- Ask some of the children to read out their stories. After each reading, the class should say what the theme of the story is. Could any of the stories have been extended further? In what way?

Extension activity

Literacy – Ask each child to choose one of their favourite books. They should write down the title of the book and the titles of the chapters. Then, tell the children to give their sheet of paper to another child. With their new sheet of chapter titles, ask the children to write their own extended story using this information. (Make sure the children haven't read the book before.)

Animal Mad

Chapter 1 – The new pet

Josh loved animals. When he was six his mum bought him a white gerbil. Josh called her Snowy. One night Snowy had five babies. Josh gave one to his friend and kept the rest. He bought them a new cage with a fancy wheel and a play tunnel.

Chapter 2 – Cats and dogs

When Josh was seven he found a stray dog. It was black and white with long ears. Josh called him Floppy. One day Josh heard Floppy barking in the garden. At the top of the tree, Josh could see something black and furry. It was a kitten. Josh climbed up the tree and took the kitten inside. His mum said he could keep it. The dog and cat became best friends and even slept in the same basket.

Chapter 3 – Ducklings

When Josh was eight he visited his uncle on the farm. His uncle showed him the new born ducklings. Josh put four in his pocket and took them home. He put them in the bath and filled it with water. Josh's dad said he could keep the ducklings. They built a large pond in the back garden so that the ducklings would have somewhere to swim.

Chapter 4 – A zoo

That wasn't the end of Josh's pets. By the time he was ten, he'd also got a rabbit, a parrot and three tortoises. Josh's mum said the house was more like a zoo and Josh agreed.

Kinaesthetic learning

(Interpersonal, Linguistic, Physical, Visual/Spatial)

Make a storyboard

- Tell the children that they are going to work in a group of four to make a large storyboard. Each child will depict a chapter of a new book called 'Sport Mad'.

- Provide each group with four pieces of ruled A4 paper, four pieces of plain A4 paper and four pieces of plain A2 paper.

- Ask the children to think of a name for the character in the story and to think of a chapter title each, for example 'Chapter 1 – Football'.

- The children should then use a copy of 'My longer story' on page 38 to plan their chapter. Ask them to write the finished chapter on the ruled paper, and the chapter number, title and an illustration of the sport on the plain paper. When they have finished, help them to stick their work onto one piece of A2 paper and write the title at the top.

Auditory learning

(Interpersonal, Musical, Linguistic)

Perform a story

- Tell the children that they are going to work in groups of four to perform an extended story with the title 'Music Mad'.

- Provide each group with a variety of musical instruments, such as a tambourine and a recorder.

- Ask the children to choose a character for the story. Each child in the group should then think of a chapter using an instrument, for example 'Chapter 1 – John bought a recorder. He wasn't very good! (Play instrument.) His mum went to the shop to buy some cotton wool for the family because they were getting earache!' The children can use copies of 'My longer story' on page 38 to plan their chapter.

- Invite the groups to perform the extended story to the rest of the class.

Visual learning

(Interpersonal, Visual/Spatial, Linguistic)

Make a concertina book

- Tell the children that they are going to work in groups to make a long concertina book called 'Magic Mad' using strips of A3 paper.

- Ask the children to think of a chapter and title, for example Chapter 1 – The magic wand, Chapter 2 – The magic box. They can use copies of 'My longer story' on page 38 to plan their chapter.

- Demonstrate how to fold the strip of paper into at least four squares. Ask the children to write their chapters on these squares.

- When everyone has finished, the chapters can be stuck together with sticky tape to make a long concertina book.

My longer story

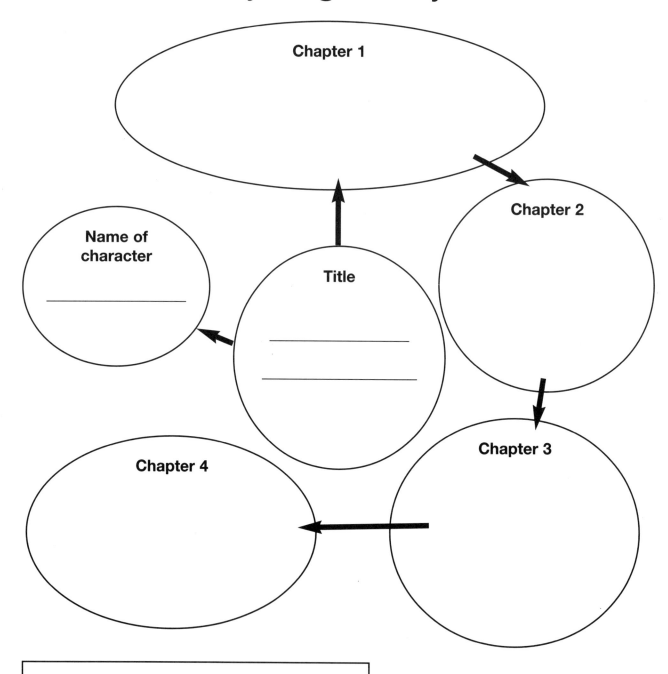

Chapter 1

Name of character
_____

Title
_____
_____

Chapter 2

Chapter 3

Chapter 4

IDEAS

Sport Mad: football, swimming, netball, rounders, tennis

Music Mad: recorder, drum, tambourine, triangle, maracas

Magic Mad: wand, card, coins, box, dice, hat

THINK ABOUT...
- A theme
- An idea for each chapter
- An ending

Poetry

Whole class starter

Literacy objective
- To write a poem with a chorus.

What you need
- Photocopies of page 41
- Photocopies of page 43
- Coloured pens, or computer and colour printer

- Give each child a copy of the poem 'Questions' on page 41 or display it on an OHP or interactive whiteboard.

- Tell the children that they are going to be looking at poems with a chorus. What is a chorus? Encourage them to share their ideas. Explain that they may have some more ideas about poems with a chorus after reading the poem together.

- Read the poem with the children. Ask them to tell you which part is the chorus. Reread it, asking them to join in the chorus.

- Ask the children the following questions about the poem.

  - What is the title of the poem?
  - What is it about?
  - Who would read a poem like this?
  - How many verses are there?
  - How many lines are there in each verse?
  - How many lines are there in the chorus?
  - Can you find the rhymes?
  - There are two different patterns for the rhymes. What are they? (Chorus – 2nd and 4th lines rhyme, verse – 1st and 2nd lines rhyme.)
  - This poem has a rhythm. What is a rhythm?
  - How does the rhythm help when you are reading the poem?

Extension activity

Literacy – Give the children a variety of poetry books and hymn books to look at, or photocopy some poems and hymns. Ask the children to highlight the choruses. How many of them rhyme? Do they prefer the poems that rhyme or not? Why?

Independent/group work

From the activities on page 42 either:

- select the most appropriate activity for each child/group according to whether they are kinaesthetic, auditory or visual learners and organise three separate working groups;

or

- begin with the kinaesthetic activity for the whole class, then progress to the auditory and finally the visual activity over several lessons.

Tell the children that they are now going to work on their own poem with a chorus.

The auditory learners will need:
copies of the bottom part of page 43.

The visual learners will need:
copies of the top part of page 43, coloured pens or a computer and colour printer.

Plenary

Share the results from the activities.

- Most people like poems with rhythm. Why do the children think that is?
- How does a rhythm help them read the poem?
- When they say a poem aloud, does it help if they have something to help them keep the rhythm? Why?
- Would they have enjoyed the poems as much if they didn't rhyme?
- Why do people like rhyming poems?

Questions

Tell me, tell me
Tell me now.
Where and when
And who and how?

Why is snow always white?
Why is there day and why is there night?

Tell me, tell me
Tell me now.
Where and when
And who and how?

Who chose the sky to be so blue?
Why is there no one quite like you?

Tell me, tell me
Tell me now.
Where and when
And who and how?

How do birds and aeroplanes fly?
What happens to us when we die?

Susan Garnett

Kinaesthetic learning

(Interpersonal, Linguistic, Physical)

Perform an action poem

- Tell the children that they are going to work in small groups to extend the poem. They will write their own ideas for the verses, which they will then act out.

- Ask each child to think of two rhyming questions for a new verse.

- Invite them to read out their poems to the others in the class using actions, for example for the line 'How do birds and aeroplanes fly?' they could flap their wings.

- Encourage the other children to join in with the actions.

Auditory learning

(Interpersonal, Linguistic, Musical)

Recite a poem

- Tell the children that they are going to work in small groups to write a poem about school. They can use this chorus to help them – 'School school, where you have fun, School school, where work's never done'.

- Ask the children to write verses that are two lines long about various aspects of school life,

for example school dinners – 'Every day we have school dinner, If you don't eat it you'll get thinner.' Give out copies of the top half of page 43 for the children to write their ideas.

- Encourage them to click their fingers or clap their hands to keep rhythm as they perform their poem.

Visual learning

(Intrapersonal, Linguistic, Visual/Spatial)

Write a poem

- Tell the children that they are going to work on their own to write a poem called 'Colour'. They can use this chorus to help them – 'Colour colour, everywhere, Makes you stand, makes you stare.'

- Give out copies of the bottom half of page 43 for the children to write their verse ideas, for

example 'Clouds are the colour white. We see them at day and we see them at night.'

- When the children have written their verses, ask them to write the poem out neatly on paper using coloured pens for the chorus. Alternatively, ask them to work at the computer and to print out the poem using different colours for the verses and the chorus.

My poem

School

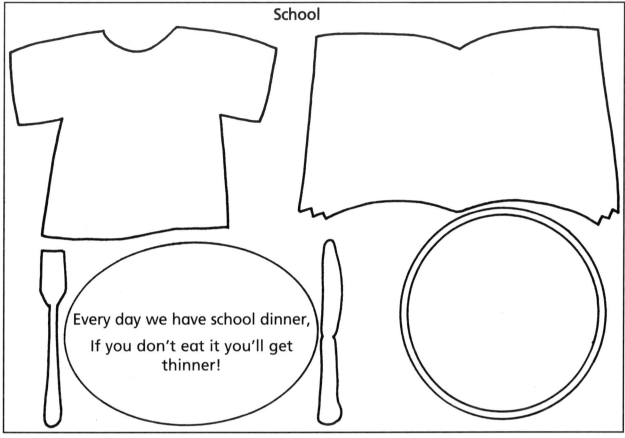

Every day we have school dinner,
If you don't eat it you'll get thinner!

Colour

Clouds are the colour white.

We see them at day and we see them at night.

Collecting information

Literacy objective

- To collect information from a variety of sources and present it as a wall chart.

What you need

- Photocopies of pages 46 (or copies enlarged to A3) and 48
- A2 paper
- Books, magazines and videos featuring cartoon characters
- Scissors and glue
- Leaves, fruit from trees etc.
- Books about trees, plus photocopies from these books
- Use of computer and Internet
- Colour printer

Whole class starter

- Give each child a copy of 'Reptiles' on page 46 (it may be more appropriate to enlarge it to A3 size so that it looks like a wall chart) or display it on an OHP or interactive whiteboard.

- Tell the children that they are going to be looking at ways of collecting information to make a wall chart. What do they think a wall chart is?

- Show them the reptiles chart and tell them that this is a wall chart about reptiles.

- Ask them the following questions.

  - Is the information fact or fiction?
  - What information is given to the reader?
  - How is it different to a story? (It has lots of factual information.)
  - How many headings are there? What are they? Why are headings needed?
  - How do headings help the reader? What would happen if you switched them around?

- Explain to the children that if they were going to make a wall chart, they would probably collect the information from different sources. What sources would they be? (For example, books, encyclopedias, magazines and the Internet.)

- Tell them they will now be working in pairs or small groups to create a wall chart.

Independent/group work

From the activities on page 47 either:

- select the most appropriate activity for each child/group according to whether they are kinaesthetic, auditory or visual learners and organise three separate working groups;

or

- begin with the kinaesthetic activity for the whole class, then progress to the auditory and finally the visual activity over several lessons.

Tell the children that they are now going to work on their own wall chart.

The kinaesthetic learners will need:
copies of 'Reptiles' on page 48, A2 paper, books, magazines and videos about cartoon characters, scissors and glue.

The auditory learners will need:
copies of 'Reptiles' on page 48, leaves, fruit, wax crayons, plain paper, books about trees, photocopies from the books, scissors and glue.

The visual learners will need:
computer and Internet access, colour printer, scissors, glue and large pieces of plain paper.

Plenary

Talk about the different sources of information the children have used.

- Which sources were the easiest to use?
- Which source provided the best information for a wall chart?
- What else could the children have used?
- Which of the wall charts were most effective? Why?
- Is presentation important?
- How do wall charts help people learn?
- How could the children improve their wall chart?

Extension activities

Cross-curricular – Ask the children to choose a topic of their own choice to research. How many sources of information can they use to make a wall chart?

Show the children a catalogue with wall charts in it. Ask the children to decide which charts would be useful to the class and why.

REPTILES

Snakes

Snakes are reptiles. They can open their mouths very wide. They swallow food whole. They smell with their tongues.

Crocodiles

Crocodiles are reptiles. They live in rivers in hot countries. They are good swimmers. They lay eggs.

Turtles

Turtles are reptiles. They have a hard shell covering their body. They spend most of their time in the sea. They lay eggs on lands.

Lizards

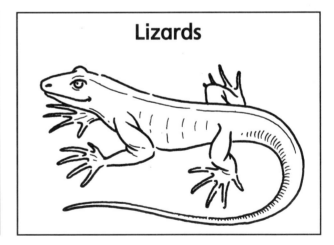

Lizards are reptiles. They live in bushes and trees. They catch insects by sticking their tongues out.

Kinaesthetic learning

(Interpersonal, Physical, Logical, Visual/Spatial, Linguistic)

Make a chart

- Tell the children that they are going to work in small groups to make a collage wall chart about cartoon characters.

- Give out copies of 'My wall chart' on page 48 for the children to make notes about what will appear on the wall chart and which sources of information may be used.

- Give each group a sheet of A2 paper, and some children's magazines, books and videos featuring cartoon characters.

- Ask the children to make a wall chart by writing the title at the top of the sheet. They should then choose four to eight cartoon characters, look through the magazines, cut out the characters and stick them on the paper with a title above each one. Underneath each picture, the children should write some information about them.

- Display the chart on the wall.

Auditory learning

(Interpersonal, Linguistic, Naturalistic, Visual/Spatial)

Show and tell

- Tell the children that they are going to work in small groups to do a 'show and tell' with information they have collected about trees.

- Ask the children to go outside to collect leaves and fruit from trees and to make rubbings (for example, bark and leaves).

- Give each group some books about trees, and allow them to make some photocopies.

- Give out copies of 'My wall chart' on page 48 for them to plan their wall chart.

- Ask the children to write the title of the chart at the top of the sheet. Then tell the children to choose four to eight trees, and to stick what they have collected about these trees onto the sheet under a relevant heading. They should also write about each tree using the information collected from the books.

- Invite the children to show the chart to the class and tell them all about it.

Visual learning

(Interpersonal, Visual/Spatial, Logical, Linguistic)

Use the Internet

- Tell the children that they are going to work in pairs to make a wall chart about a country of their choice using information from the Internet.

- First, the children should make notes on what kind of information they are going to look for.

Then ask them to locate the information on the Internet and then print it out.

- Ask the children to write the title of the chart at the top of a large sheet of plain paper and then to write between four and eight headings under which they should stick some of the information (for example, pictures and maps). They could write information underneath.

- Display the chart on the wall.

My wall chart

Title _____

Sources of information

_____

_____

_____

_____

_____

THINK ABOUT...
- Where you will get your information
- What pictures you will have
- How you will present your information

Headings

_____

_____

_____

_____

_____

_____

_____

_____

_____

_____

Pictures

Dilemmas

Literacy objective

- To write a story about a dilemma and the issues it raises for the character.

What you need

- Photocopies of pages 51, 53 and 54
- Ruled and plain paper
- Sticky tape
- Word-processing computer program

Whole class starter

- Give each child a copy of the story 'Don't do it!' on page 51 or display it on an OHP or interactive whiteboard.

- Tell the children that they are going to work on dilemmas. Have they heard the word 'dilemma' before? What does it mean? Do not tell them the answer yet – wait until they've read the story.

- Read the story 'Don't do it!' with the children. Tell them that this is a story about a dilemma. Explain that a dilemma is when someone has to make a choice between two undesirable alternatives.

- Ask the children the following questions.

  – What is the dilemma in the story?
  – What would happen if Jack did it?
  – What would happen if he didn't do it?
  – How do you think Jack felt?
  – What would you do?
  – What other dilemmas are children faced with?

- Write a list of dilemmas on the board, such as stealing, telling lies, damaging something and hurting someone. Talk about each one individually. The children may wish to share their experiences although some tact may be needed.

Extension activity

Literacy – Ask the children to write a concertina book about a dilemma. They could use pictures, and they must write two different endings. Tell them to give their finished story to a partner. Which ending would the partner choose? Why?

Independent/group work

From the activities on page 53 either:

- select the most appropriate activity for each child/group according to whether they are kinaesthetic, auditory or visual learners and organise three separate working groups;

or

- begin with the kinaesthetic activity for the whole class, then progress to the auditory and finally the visual activity over several lessons.

Tell the children that they are now going to work on dilemmas.

The kinaesthetic learners will need:
copies of the dilemmas on page 54, ruled paper, plain paper and sticky tape.

The auditory learners will need:
the dilemmas on page 54 (for the teacher).

The visual learners will need:
copies of pages 53 'My dilemma' and 54 'Dilemmas'.

Plenary

Share the results from the activities.

- What choices did the children make? Why?
- Of the choices they made, which do the others feel would be the most appropriate?
- How can the children avoid getting into those dilemmas?
- What dilemmas will they have to face in the future? (For example, going to secondary school or when they are an adult.) Share some of these dilemmas and their possible solutions.
- Discuss the following scenarios. What would happen if:
  - they made the wrong choice and got into trouble with the police, their parents or teachers;
  or
  - they made the right choice and lost their friends or were bullied.

Don't do it!

Jack and his family had moved to the other side of town. Jack was fed up. He had changed schools and hadn't made any friends.

One Saturday afternoon, as he was walking through the park, he saw some boys from his school. He got chatting to them and had a game of football with them. As he was about to go, Tom, the leader of the gang, grabbed his arm.

'If you want to be in our gang, meet us here tonight,' said Tom. 'We're going to have some fun!'

'I can't,' said Jack. 'I have to be home for eight.'

The boys looked at one another and laughed.

'You're not a mummy's boy are you?' growled Tom.

'No, no,' said Jack, afraid. 'Okay, I'll come.'

It was dark when Jack arrived. The gang was waiting. Together they ran across the park to a quiet street of houses and stopped at the end of the street.

'If you want to be in our gang, you've got to knock on three of the houses in this street and then run off,' said Tom.

Jack looked at the boys. They were serious. He knew it was wrong.

If he did it he might get caught and the people might call the police but if he didn't do it, then the gang would probably beat him up.

'Go on do it,' said Tom giving Jack a push.

Nervously, Jack set off up the path to the first front door. He stopped on the doorstep and turned to look at the boys. What should he do?

Kinaesthetic learning
(Intrapersonal, Visual/Spatial, Physical, Linguistic)

Make a flap book
- Tell the children that they are going to make a flap book story about a dilemma. Give them the list of dilemmas (page 54) and ask them to choose one or choose one for them.

- Give each child a sheet of ruled paper and two small sheets of plain paper half the width of the ruled sheet. Ask them to write 'Do it!' on one piece of plain paper and 'Don't do it!' on the other.

- They should write their story on the ruled sheet of paper. At the bottom of the page, ask them to draw a line down the middle of the page. They should write one ending on the left-hand side of the line and the other on the right-hand side.

- Show the children how to tape the two pieces of paper onto the bottom of the ruled sheet to make flaps that cover the endings.

- Invite the children to read out their stories up to the ending. Ask other children to pick one of the choices and read it.

Auditory learning
(Interpersonal, Linguistic, Logical)

Circle time
- Seat the children in a circle.

- Tell the children a dilemma from the list provided on page 54.

- In turn, ask the children what they would do about the dilemma. Encourage them to give reasons for their choices.

- After you have gone round the circle, ask the children to choose the best solution to the dilemma.

- Repeat with another dilemma from the list.

- They should write up one of the dilemmas in their exercise book or on paper.

Visual learning
(Intrapersonal, Linguistic, Visual/Spatial)

Word processing
- Tell the children they are going to work on their own to write a dilemma using a word processor on the computer.

- Give out copies of pages 53 'My dilemma' and 54 'Dilemmas'. Ask the children to choose a dilemma from page 54 (or choose one for them) and, in note form, complete the necessary information about it on page 53.

- They should then write up the details on a computer. When they get to the two choices they are going to make and the consequences, they should use two different colours on the computer.

- If possible, these should be printed out on colour printers for the rest of the class to read.

My dilemma

The dilemma

_____

_____

_____

THINK ABOUT...
- The setting
- Who it happens to
- What the choices are and the consequences

Where it happens

_____

Who with

_____

Choice 1 and consequence

_____

_____

_____

_____

Choice 2 and consequence

_____

_____

_____

_____

Dilemmas

Your friends are smoking. They want you to do it, too.
You could join them or you could say no.

What do you do?

You have left your homework at home.
You could copy from a friend, say the dog's eaten it or you could tell the truth.

What do you do?

You have lost your friend's watch and they want it back.
You could steal money from home to pay for another or you could tell them you've lost it.

What do you do?

Your friends are going to take the day off school because the fair is in town. You could go with them or you could say no and go to school.

What do you do?

You have got a really bad report at school.
You could rip it up and not take it home or you could take it home as it is.

What do you do?

Alternative endings

Literacy objective

- To create an alternative ending for a known story.

What you need

- Photocopies of page 57 and 59
- Accessories for dressing up (for example, coat, glasses, hat, tie)
- A tape recorder/dictaphone

Whole class starter

- Give each child a copy of 'George's Marvellous Medicine (the other version!)' on page 57 or display it on an OHP or interactive whiteboard.

- Tell the children that they are going to work on alternative endings. Ask if any of them know what that means. Write their ideas on the board.

- Read the alternative ending with the children. Tell them that this is the alternative ending to *George's Marvellous Medicine* by Roald Dahl. If they have not read the story, give them a summary of it.

- Ask the children the following questions.

  - Who were the characters in the story?
  - Which characters were good and which characters were bad? How do you know?
  - Why do you think George had given Grandma the medicine?
  - Who wanted to give Grandma another chance? Why?
  - What animal did George try the medicine on?
  - What do you think happened to the animal?
  - What happened to Grandma when she drank the medicine?
  - Why was George happy?
  - How was this ending different to the real story? Which do you prefer? Why?
  - What other Roald Dahl books do you know?
  - What always happens to the bad characters in his books?
  - If you were writing an alternative ending to one of his books, how could you change this?

Independent/group work

From the activities on page 58 either:

- select the most appropriate activity for each child/group according to whether they are kinaesthetic, auditory or visual learners and organise three separate working groups;

or

- begin with the kinaesthetic activity for the whole class, then progress to the auditory and finally the visual activity over several lessons.

Tell the children that they are now going to work on alternative endings.

The kinaesthetic learners will need:
copies of 'Alternative endings' on page 59 and accessories for dressing up, such as glasses, a scarf and a jacket.

The auditory learners will need:
a tape recorder or dictaphone.

The visual learners will need:
copies of 'Alternative endings' on page 59.

Plenary

Share the results from the activities.

- Which were the most successful alternative endings? Why?
- Were the new endings better than the original?
- Were the best endings always the happiest?
- Which children preferred a sad/happy ending?
- Why is the ending important?

How will this work help the children in their future writing, i.e. trying to think of an ending the reader will not expect. Ask the children to look at previous work they have done. Look at their endings. How could they be improved?

George's Marvellous Medicine

(the other version!)

George didn't like his grandma. She was a mean old woman. So he made a magic medicine and turned her into a giant.

George's mum felt sorry for Grandma.

'Give her another chance,' said Mum. 'She's an old lady. She doesn't mean to be so nasty.'

'Okay,' said George, smiling to himself.

George went inside and made a new medicine. He tested it on a hen. It worked. Then he ran outside and called Grandma.

'Grandma, I've got some medicine to make you better,' he shouted.

Grandma appeared from behind the house.

'Hurry up George!' she replied in her bad-tempered way.

George winked at his mother as he gave Grandma the new medicine. She snatched it from his hands and drank it down in one. In a matter of just one second, she began shrinking! She shrank to the size of the house, then the apple tree and soon she was back to normal, except for one thing. It wasn't just her size that had shrunk. George smiled.

'Why are you smiling?' asked his mum.

'Ask Grandma,' said George winking.

'Grandma, how are you feeling?' asked Mum.

Grandma's mouth opened, but no sound came out.

'Speak up!' said Mum. 'I can't hear what you're saying.'

Grandma tried again and although she moved her lips no sound came out.

'I didn't just shrink her body, I shrank her voice, too!' said George, smiling.

George and his mum laughed as Grandma continued to moan, but not a word came from her lips.

'Perfect,' said George happily. 'The perfect medicine.'

Kinaesthetic learning

(Interpersonal, Physical, Linguistic, Logical)

Write a TV news report

- Tell the children that they are going to work in a group to write the alternative ending of a well-known book for a television news report.

- Ask the children to discuss the new ending for a book (it must be a novel all the children know). They can write down their ideas on a copy of page 59.

- Ask the children to show the new ending as a television news report. One of the children should be the newsreader, sitting behind a desk (like in a real television studio). The others in the group should be the characters. (Provide some dressing-up clothes for them to get in role.) The newsreader should explain the new ending and then ask the characters to comment on it.

Auditory learning

(Interpersonal, Linguistic, Physical)

Play consequences

- Tell the children that they are going to play a game called 'Consequences' using a story book they know.

- Provide a dictaphone or tape recorder.

- Seat the children in a circle. Remind them of the ending to the story. Now go back in the book to a critical moment. Tell the children they are going to change it from that point in the story and that it will have consequences for what happens next.

- Start them off by taping the first sentence in the revised ending then pass the tape on.

- They take turns to pass the tape on to the next child who says the next part of the story and so on until the story is finished.

- Ask the children to play back the tape and write down the story.

Visual learning

(Intrapersonal, Linguistic, Visual/Spatial)

Make an arrow chart

- Tell the children that they are going to work on their own to write the new ending for a Roald Dahl story.

- Give out copies of 'Alternative endings' on page 59. Ask the children to fill in the name of their chosen book and the author. Then tell

them to write the first sentence of the ending on the first line, and so on, until the story is finished.

- Invite the children to read out their new endings.

Alternative endings

Book _____

Author _____

The real ending

and ↓ then

and ↓ then

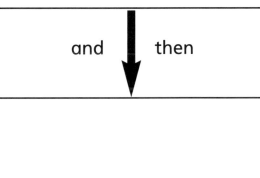

My ending

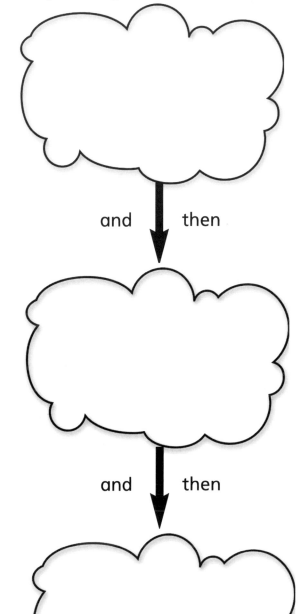

and ↓ then

and ↓ then

THE END!

Points of view

Literacy objective

- To plan the presentation of a point of view.

What you need

- Photocopies of pages 62 and 64
- Dressing-up clothes and accessories (such as hat, tie, glasses, jacket)
- OHT sheets
- OHT coloured pens

Whole class starter

- Give each child a copy of 'School holidays' on page 62 or display it on an OHP or interactive whiteboard.

- Tell the children that they are going to work on points of view. Ask if any of them know what a point of view means. Write their definitions on the blackboard.

- Read 'School holidays' with the children. Tell them that this is not a story but a report that contains a collection of points of view.

- Ask the children the following questions.

  – What is the information about?
  – Who has collected the information?
  – Will the information be read by people or heard? How do you know?
  – How many people's points of view are there?

- Write two lists on the board with the headings 'For' and 'Against'. Ask the children what should be written in each column using the information they have read.

  – How many people are for school holidays and how many are against them?
  – Do the children agree with any of the people? Why?

- Tell the children that, when writing up a point of view, it is important to back up your point of view with evidence. Can they find any evidence in the different points of view in 'School holidays'? Which person has the most conclusive evidence?

Independent/group work

From the activities on page 63 either:

- select the most appropriate activity for each child/group according to whether they are kinaesthetic, auditory or visual learners and organise three separate working groups;

or

- begin with the kinaesthetic activity for the whole class, then progress to the auditory and finally the visual activity over several lessons.

Tell the children that they are now going to work on points of view.

The kinaesthetic learners will need:
dressing-up clothes and accessories (such as hat, jacket, tie, glasses) and copies of 'My point of view' on page 64.

The auditory learners will need:
copies of 'My point of view' on page 64.

The visual learners will need:
copies of 'My point of view' on page 64, OHT sheets and OHT coloured pens.

Plenary

Share the results from the activities.

- Is it easier to express a point of view on paper or verbally? Ask the children for their opinions.

- Ask the children to share their points of view. Write down the 'fors' and 'againsts'. Which do they agree with and why?

- Ask the children to give evidence to back up their views. Why is evidence important?

- In which professions would evidence be needed? (Lawyer, politican, police.)

Extension activity

Literacy – Give the children a selection of newspapers and/or magazines. Ask them to read through some of the stories that express a point of view. Tell the children to cut out one of the stories that interests them. They should then stick the report on a piece of paper and write their own point of view underneath.

School holidays

'Good morning everyone, this is Lee Moss on Radio KLC. Well it's another hot sunny day and all the kids are happy because it's the school holidays. But what do other people think about the summer holidays? We've been out and about talking to people in the town. Are summer holidays a good thing or bad thing? Let's find out.'

Mrs Jane Green, wife and mother

'I think the summer holidays should be shorter. I have two children and work full time. During the summer holidays it is difficult finding someone to look after the children. I had to put an advert in the paper four times before I found a child minder.'

Miss Claire Short, teacher

'I am a teacher and I need the long summer holidays to recover from a hard term's work. Children are tired too and need the break.'

Mr Paul Hirst, shopkeeper

'I make a lot more money during the holidays. The children are in and out of the shop all day buying things. The long summer holidays are a great idea.'

PC Tom Brown

'We have a lot of problems with children during the summer holidays. There's a lot more vandalism. At least 20 cases were reported in just one week last summer. There are more accidents involving children, too. I think the summer holidays should be shorter.'

Kinaesthetic learning

(Interpersonal, Linguistic, Physical)

Hot seating

- Tell the children that they are going to be involved in 'hot seating' in order to discuss the school curriculum – whether the subjects they do are necessary and what other subjects should be taught.

- Tell the children that they are going to take on the role of different characters putting across their point of view, for example a headteacher, the Prime Minister, a businessman and child. Decide which role each child is going to take and let them choose dressing-up clothes and/or accessories to help them get in role.

- Ask the children to make notes on a copy of page 64 about what their character may say.

- When the children have practised saying their point of view, invite them to sit in the hot seat (in a special chair) and take on the role of that person. The rest of the class can ask them questions.

Auditory learning

(Interpersonal, Logical, Physical)

School council meeting

- Tell the children that they are going to work together to discuss whether sport in school is necessary.

- Invite them to imagine that they are at a school council meeting. Ask them to elect a chairman, and a secretary to take notes.

- Hand out copies of page 64 for the children to make notes on their point of view.

- Stage a school council discussion where the children can talk about their points of view. When they have discussed all their reasons, nominate a spokesperson to inform the rest of the class. Ask the other children for their opinions.

Visual learning

(Intrapersonal, Linguistic, Visual/Spatial, Logical)

Produce an OHT

- Tell the children that they are going to work on their own to produce an OHT about residential holidays.

- Ask each child to think of reasons why they are for or against residential holidays. They can make notes about their point of view on a copy of 'My point of view' on page 64.

- Give the children OHT sheets and coloured OHT pens to present their point of view on an OHP.

- Invite them to show their finished OHTs in a presentation to the rest of the class.

My point of view

Advertisements

Literacy objective

- To design an advertisement.

What you need

- Photocopies of pages 67 and 69
- Empty plastic bottles and/or drink cans
- Paper
- Coloured pens
- Scissors and glue
- Large sheets of paper

Whole class starter

- Give each child a copy of the advertisement 'Robot House Cleaner' on page 67 or display it on an OHP or interactive whiteboard.

- Tell the children that they are going to work on advertisements.

- Read the advertisement with the children. Ask them the following questions.

  - What is the advertisement for?
  - Why would people want to buy something like this?
  - How does the writer tempt the reader?
  - Would you buy this cleaner?
  - The writer exaggerates what the cleaner can do. How does he do this?
  - Why do you think the writer uses questions?
  - Why do you think there isn't a price?

- Together look at the different design devices the designer has used, such as the different type faces and fonts, and the size of the text. There are different type sizes, some of which are in capitals and others in bold. How does this help the advertisement? (If the type was all the same size it would be boring to read.)

Extension activity

Literacy – Give the children a selection of catalogues that show children's toys and games. Ask the children to choose some of the toys, cut out their pictures, and stick them onto separate pieces of paper. They should then write an advert for the toys pictured using the advertising strategies they have learned.

Independent/group work

From the activities on page 68 either:

- select the most appropriate activity for each child/group according to whether they are kinaesthetic, auditory or visual learners and organise three separate working groups;

or

- begin with the kinaesthetic activity for the whole class, then progress to the auditory and finally the visual activity over several lessons.

Tell the children they are now going to work on an advertisement of their own.

The kinaesthetic learners will need:
empty plastic bottles or drink cans, paper, coloured pens, crayons and pastels, A3/A4 paper.

The auditory learners will need:
copies of 'My advertisement' on page 69.

The visual learners will need:
copies of 'My advertisement' on page 69, large sheets of paper and felt-tipped pens and crayons.

Plenary

Share the results from the activities.

- Which are the most successful adverts?
- Why are they successful?
- What strategies are used to sell products? For example:
  - descriptive words
  - questions
  - exaggerations
  - size of type
  - type of font
  - drawings
  - colour

Robot House Cleaner

- Are you tired of cleaning?
- Are you fed up of vacuuming?
- Are you weary of dusting?

We have the answer for you!

ROBOT HOUSE CLEANER!

Robot House Cleaner will have your house cleaned in a jiffy. In the time it takes to make a cup of tea, you'll be sitting with your feet up in a beautiful clean house.

Robot House Cleaner can vacuum and dust the whole house in just two minutes. Just plug it in and off it goes.

NEW on the market today!!
Guaranteed for three years. Get one now before stocks run out. You know you can't do without it!

Tel 01643 385329 for a free demonstration.

Kinaesthetic learning

(Physical, Visual/Spatial, Intrapersonal, Linguistic)

Design it

- Tell the children that they are going to design an advertisement for a drink for children.

- Give each child a variety of drinks cans and bottles to look at. Discuss the words, shapes and colours of the lettering. Which do they think are best?

- Now ask the children to design their own advertisement for one of the drinks on A3 or A4 paper. They should draw their can/bottle on the paper and write the name of it at the top.

- Next they should think of words and phrases to advertise the drink, such as 'The fizziest pop in the word' or 'the fruitiest taste'.

- Encourage them to use a range of coloured pens, wax crayons and pastels and to include exciting words in their descriptions.

Auditory learning

(Intrapersonal, Interpersonal, Linguistic)

Make sales talk

- Tell the children that they are going to work on their own and imagine that they are a door-to-door salesperson handing out details of a super new cleaning product.

- Hand out copies of page 69 for them to use to develop the idea of the cleaning product and its unique selling points.

- Invite the children to give their sales talk to the rest of the class.

- Would the other children buy the product? Discuss reasons why or why not.

Visual learning

(Interpersonal, Linguistic, Visual/Spatial)

Produce a poster

- Tell the children that they are going to work in pairs to produce a poster advertising something to help a child.

- Hand out copies of 'My advertisement' on page 69 for them to use to develop their ideas.

- Tell the children to think of a name for the new product and to write a description of it using lots of exciting words.

- Finally, ask the children to draw a coloured picture of the new product.

My advertisement

My product

Questions to ask the buyer

Words to describe my product

 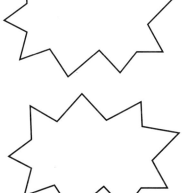 

Why you should buy it

SUPER CLEANING PRODUCT

- Fabulous fly spray
- Powerful pot washer
- Brilliant bath cleaner
- Crazy clothes ironer
- Wonderful wash powder

CHILD HELPER
- Clothes dresser
- Room tidier
- Homework help
- Hair washer

NOTES

NOTES

NOTES